ABCs

LETTER
& NUMBER
SHAPE MAZES

B is for Bible

The Bible is a special book with many stories about God and His love.

B

5 is for loaves of bread

Jesus used five loaves of bread to feed a huge crowd of people, showing that He can do great things with just a little!

5

five

EASY

Bible Activity

Book for Kids 3-5

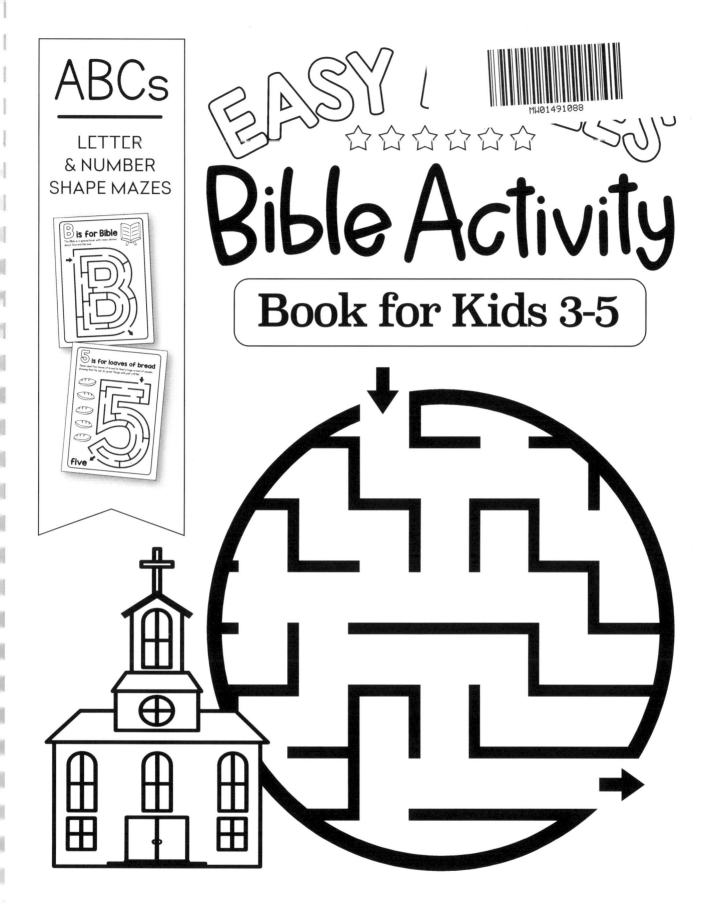

A is for Adam

Adam was the first man, and he lived in a beautiful garden called Eden.

B is for Bible

The Bible is a special book with many stories about God and His love.

C is for Cross

The cross is where Jesus showed His love by giving His life for us.

D is for David

David was a brave young boy who became a king.
He is famous for beating a giant with just a stone!

E is for Easter

Easter is the day we celebrate Jesus coming back to life, showing us that love is stronger than anything.

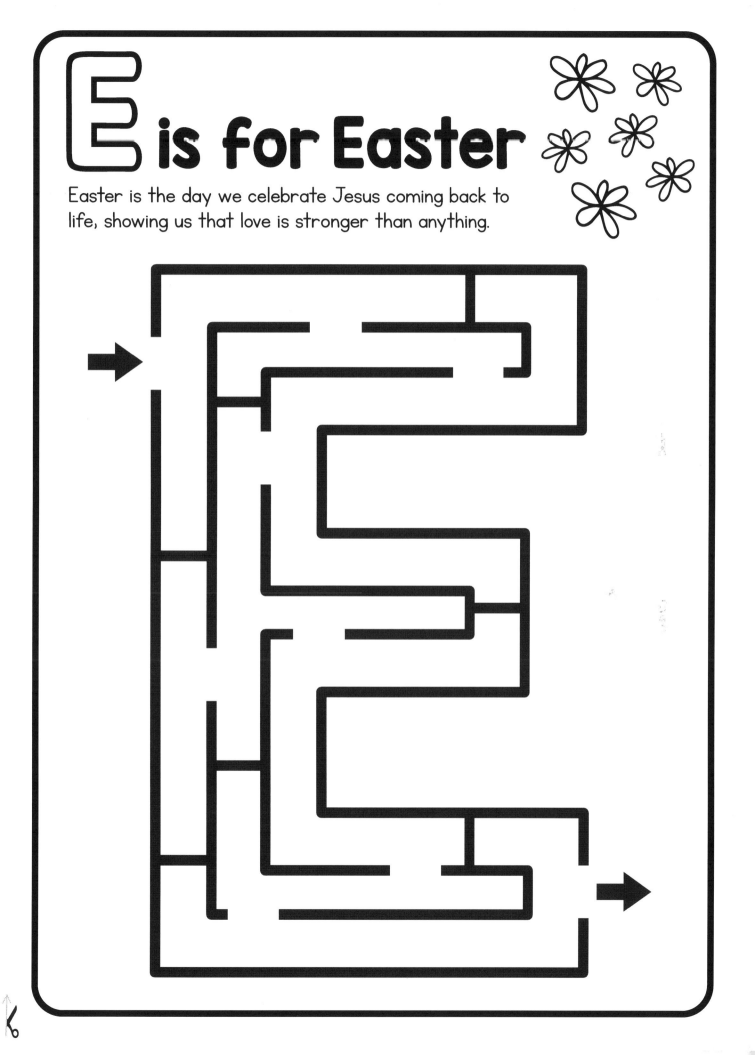

F is for Fish

Fish remind us of when Jesus fed a big crowd with just two fish and five loaves of bread.

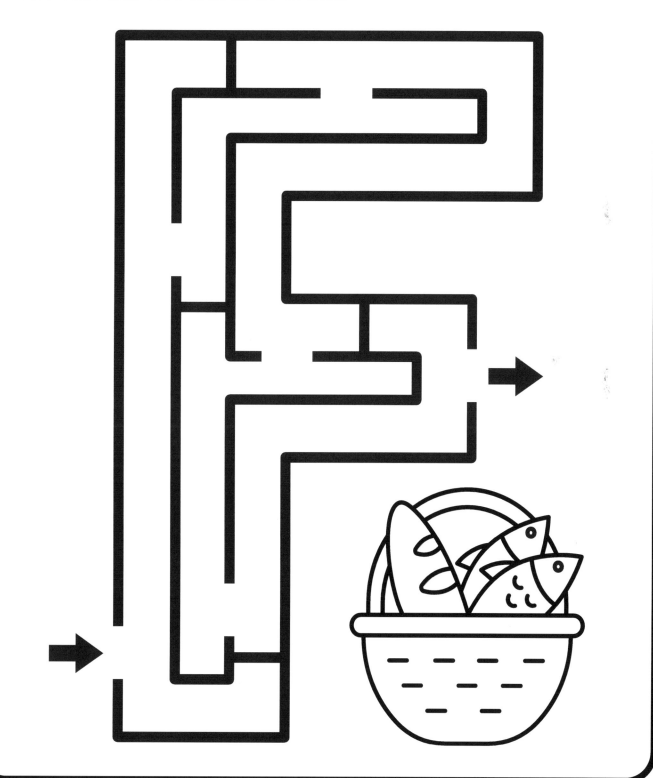

G is for God's Earth

God made our beautiful Earth with plants, animals, and people to take care of it.

H is for Heaven

Heaven is a wonderful place where God lives. It's full of joy and beauty.

I is for Israel

Israel is a special country in many Bible stories. It's where many people from the Bible lived.

J is for Jesus

Jesus is God's Son who loves everyone and teaches us how to be kind.

K is for King

In the Bible, a king is a leader chosen by God to guide and protect His people.

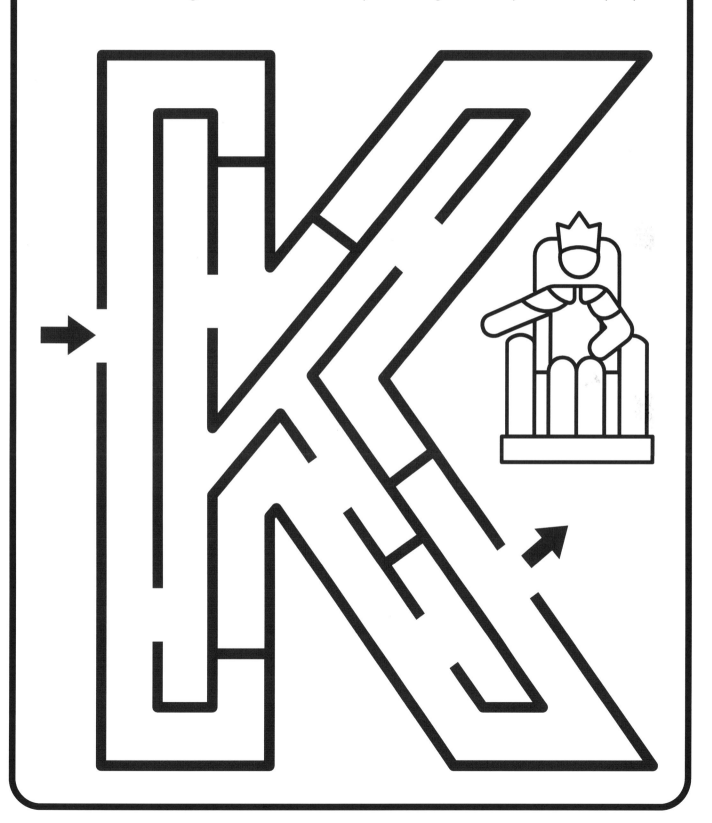

L is for Lamb

A lamb in the Bible is a symbol of gentleness and peace.
Jesus is called the Lamb of God because He brings peace.

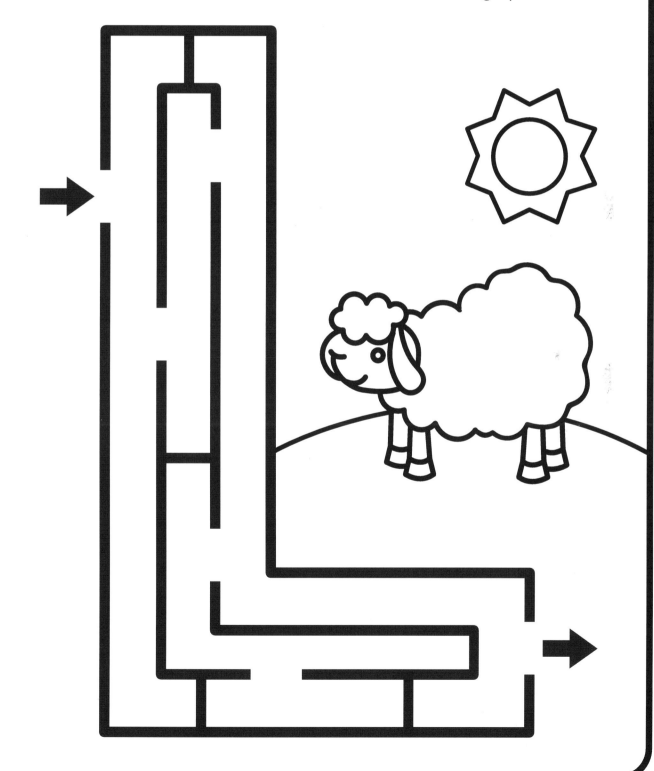

M is for Moses

Moses was a leader who helped his people travel through a big desert to find a safe home.

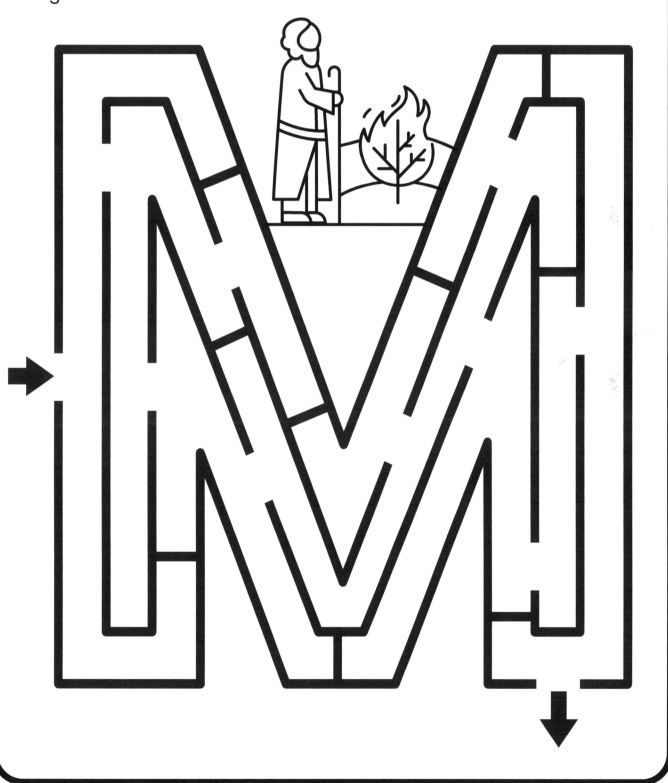

N is for Noah's Ark

Noah's Ark was a big boat that Noah built to save his family and animals from a great flood.

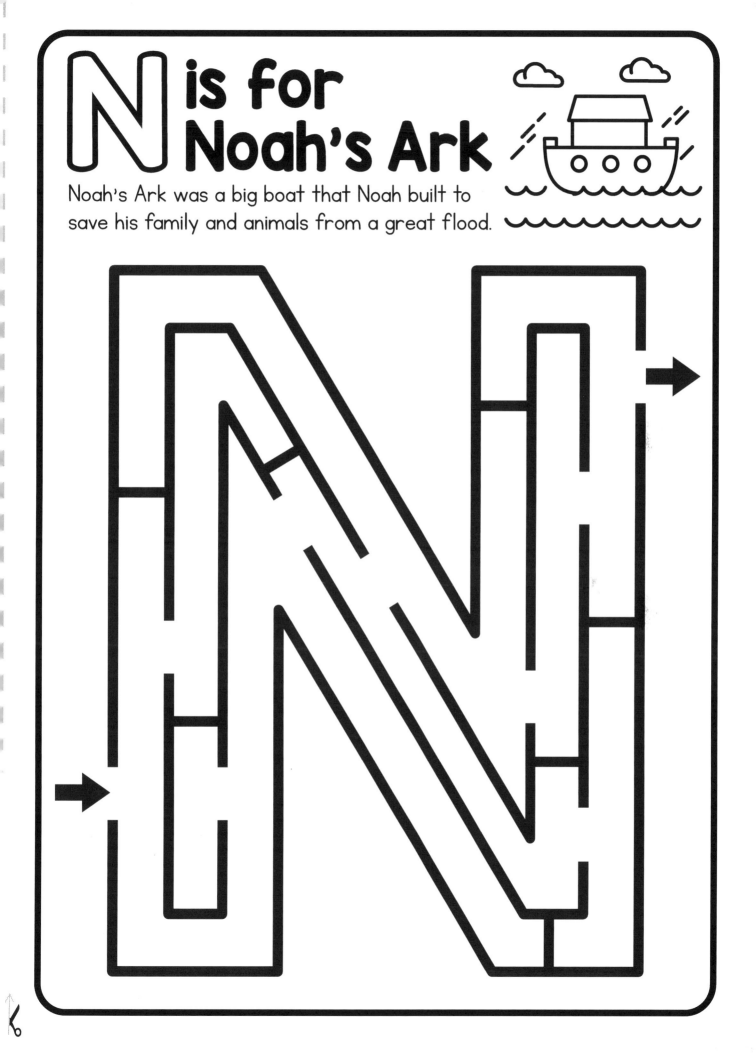

O is for Olive Branch

An olive branch is a sign of peace. Noah knew the flood was over when a dove brought him an olive branch.

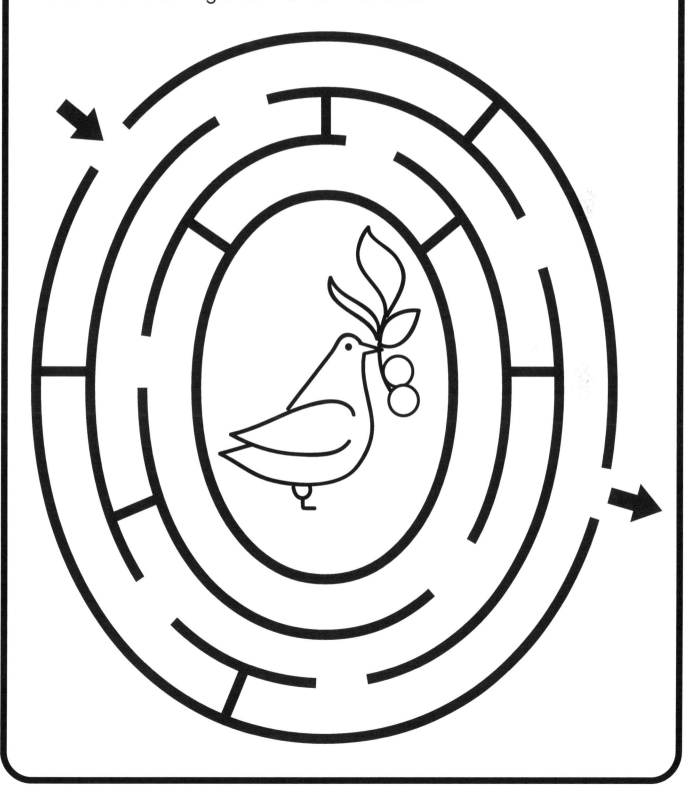

P is for Pray

Pray means talking to God. You can tell Him about your day, ask for help, or say thank you.

Q is for Queen Esther

Queen Esther was brave and saved her people by speaking up at the right time.

R is for Rainbow

A rainbow appeared in the sky as a promise from God to Noah that He would never flood the whole earth again.

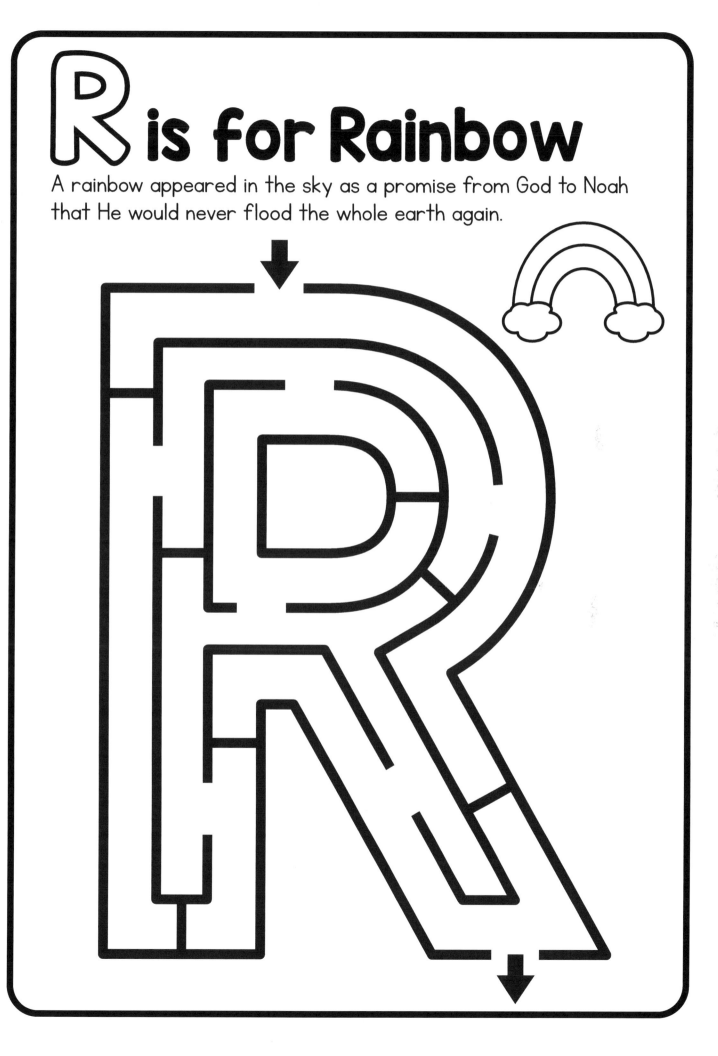

S is for Savior

Savior is a name for Jesus because He came to save people by loving them and teaching them how to live well.

T is for Trinity

The Trinity means God is three-in-one: the Father, the Son (Jesus), and the Holy Spirit, all together as one God.

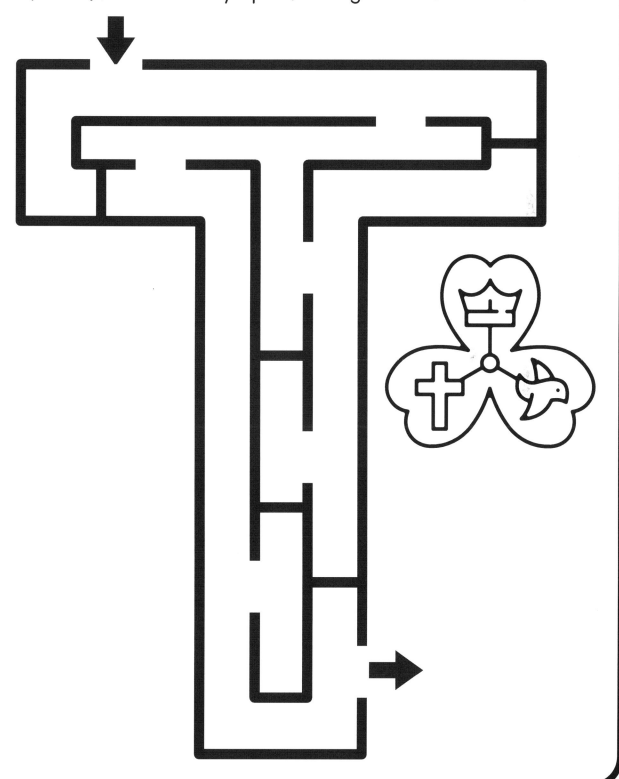

U is for Unity

Unity means being together as one. The Bible teaches us to live in harmony and love one another.

V is for Vine

Jesus said He is the vine and we are the branches.
If we stay connected to Him, we will grow strong and healthy.

W is for Jonah and the Whale

A whale swallowed Jonah when he tried to run away, but it kept him safe until he was ready to do what God asked.

X is for Crucifix

A crucifix shows Jesus on the cross, reminding us of His love and how He gave His life for us.

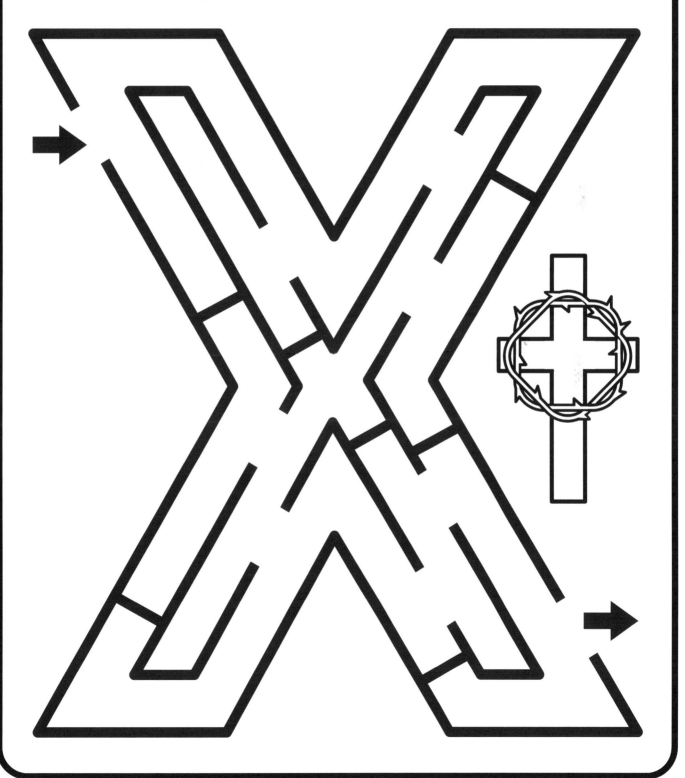

Y is for Yahweh

Yahweh is a special name for God in the Bible. It reminds us that God is always with us and cares for us.

Z is for Zion

Zion is a special hill in the city of Jerusalem, important in many Bible stories as a place of God's protection.

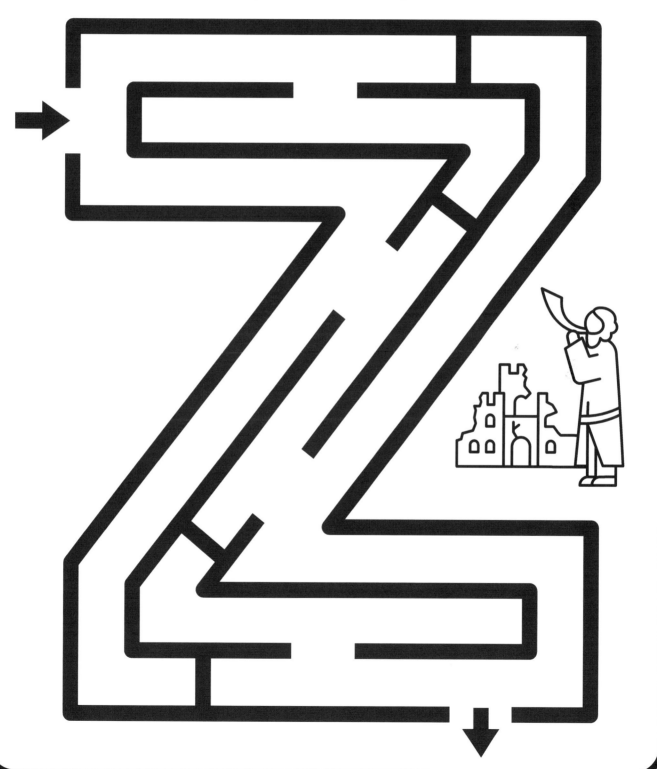

Windows in the Church

The church is getting a beautiful new stained glass window with a cross! Help guide the window through the maze so they can be put in place and make the church look even more special.

Following Jesus

This child wants to learn about Jesus and His great love. Help guide the child through the maze to find Jesus, who is waiting to share His stories and love.

Trip to Bethlehem

Mary and Joseph need to travel to Bethlehem for a very important event—the birth of Baby Jesus! Help them find the safest path through the maze to reach Bethlehem in time.

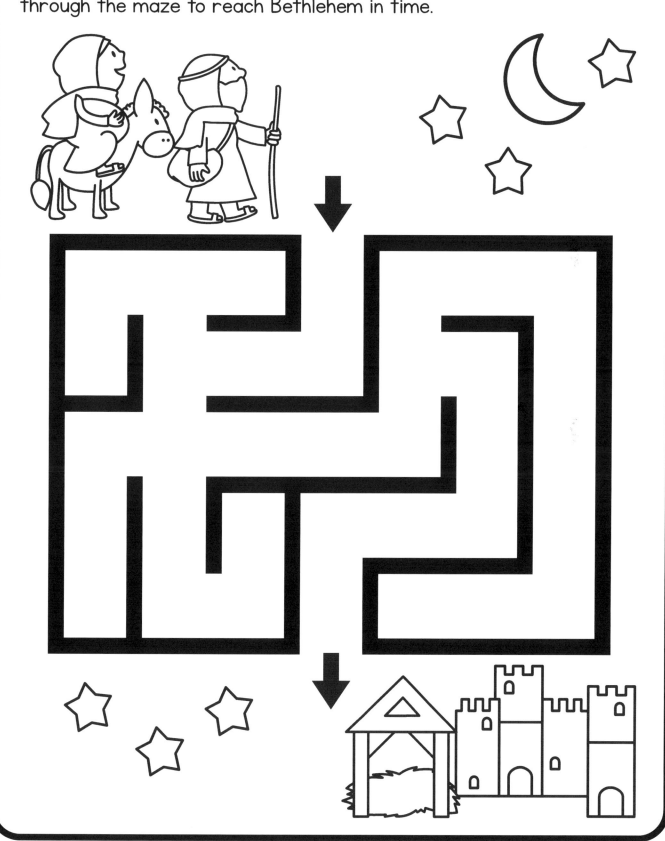

Dove Finds the Ark

After a long rain, Noah sent a dove to find dry land. The dove needs help finding its way back to Noah's Ark with an olive branch. Can you guide the dove through the maze?

David Versus Goliath

David is a young shepherd with a big heart and a slingshot. He needs to find Goliath to protect his people. Help David navigate the maze to meet Goliath for their big challenge!

Taking Communion

Some children are ready to take communion and remember Jesus's love. They need to find their way to the bread and juice. Help guide the children through the maze to reach the communion elements!

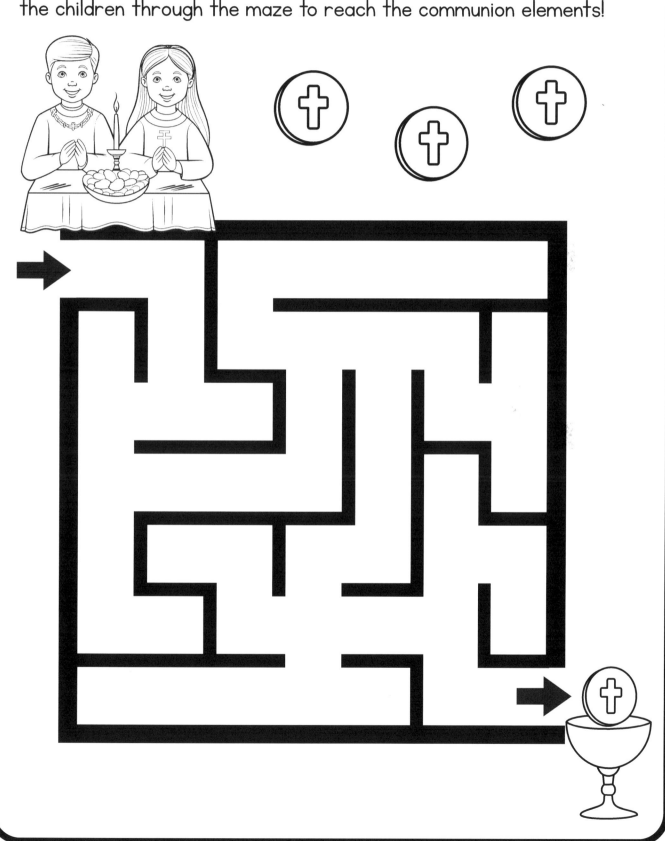

Going to Church

The children are excited to go to church and learn more about God's love. They need to find the right path to get there. Help guide the children through the maze so they can reach church on time!

The Lost Sheep

A shepherd has many sheep, but one little sheep is lost. He loves all his sheep and wants to keep them safe. Help the shepherd find his way through the maze to bring his lost sheep back home!

The Angel Gabriel

Angel Gabriel had an important message to give Mary. He needed to tell her that she would be the mother of Baby Jesus. Help Gabriel find his way through the maze to deliver his special news to Mary!

Three Wise Men

The Three Wise Men followed a bright star to find Baby Jesus. They wanted to give Him special gifts because He was a very special baby. Help them find their way through the maze to meet Baby Jesus!

O is for the empty tomb

The stone in front of Jesus' tomb was rolled away, and the tomb was empty because Jesus came back to life to show His love for us!

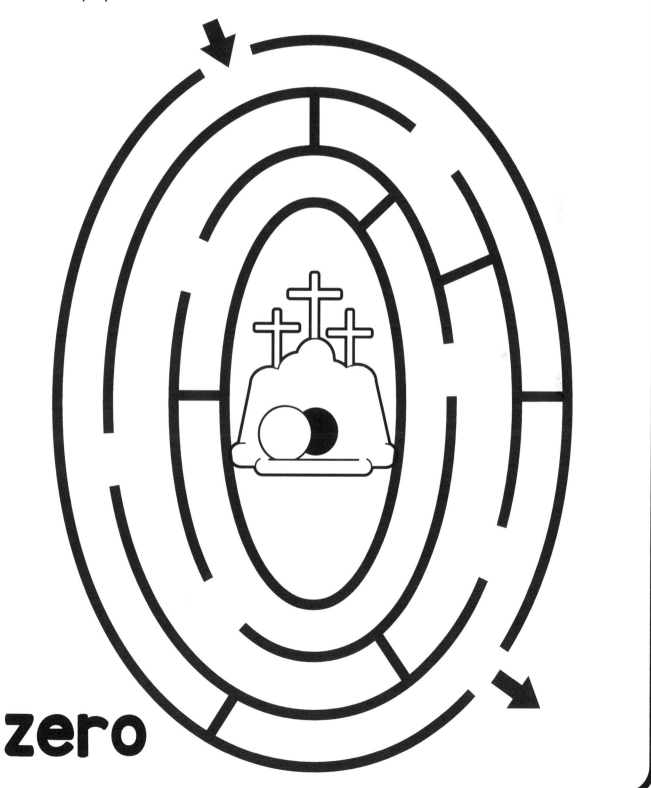

zero

1 is for one God

The number 1 reminds us there is only one God. He created everything and loves everyone very much.

one

2 is for Noah's animals

Noah saved two of every kind of animal by bringing them onto his big boat, the ark, to keep them safe from the flood.

two

3 is for the Holy Trinity

The number 3 teaches us about the Holy Trinity: God the Father, God the Son, and God the Holy Spirit. They are three parts but all one God.

three

4 is for the four Gospels

The Four Gospels are special books in the Bible that tell us all about the life of Jesus and the loving things He did. (Matthew, Mark, Luke, John)

four

5 is for loaves of bread

Jesus used five loaves of bread to feed a huge crowd of people, showing that He can do great things with just a little!

five

6 is for six water pots

At a big wedding, Jesus turned water into wine using six water pots. It was His first miracle, showing His power and kindness.

six

7 is for creation of world

God made the whole world in six days — land, sea, plants, animals, and people — and on the seventh day, He rested to show us that rest is good.

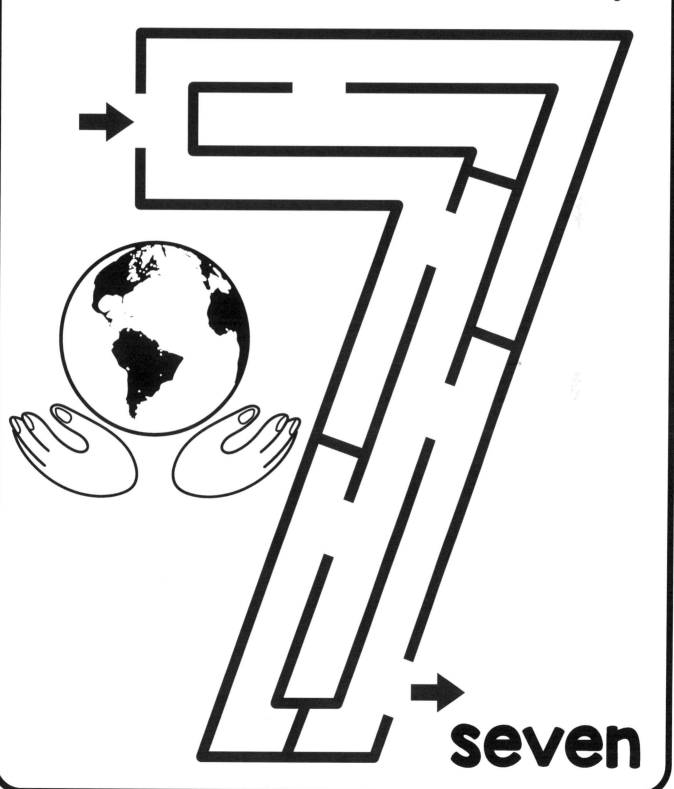

seven

8 is for people on the Ark

The number 8 reminds us of Noah's Ark, where Noah, his wife, their three sons, and their wives–eight people in total–were safe from the great flood.

eight

q is for Fruits of the Spirit

The Fruits of the Spirit are qualities that grow in us when we follow Jesus. They are love, joy, peace, patience, kindness, goodness, faithfulness, gentleness, and self-control.

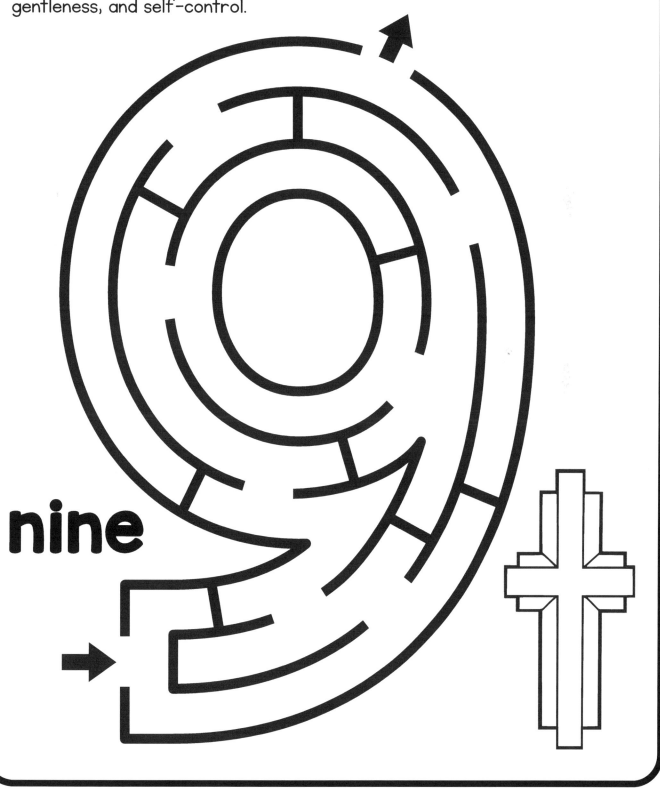

nine

10 is for the Ten Commandments

The Ten Commandments are rules God gave to help us love Him
and each other. They teach us to be kind, honest, and thankful.

ten

Made in United States
Troutdale, OR
07/20/2024

21436649R00055